Indonesian Cookbook

Discover True South East Asian Cooking with Delicious Indonesian Recipes

By
BookSumo Press

Published by
http://www.booksumo.com

LEGAL NOTES

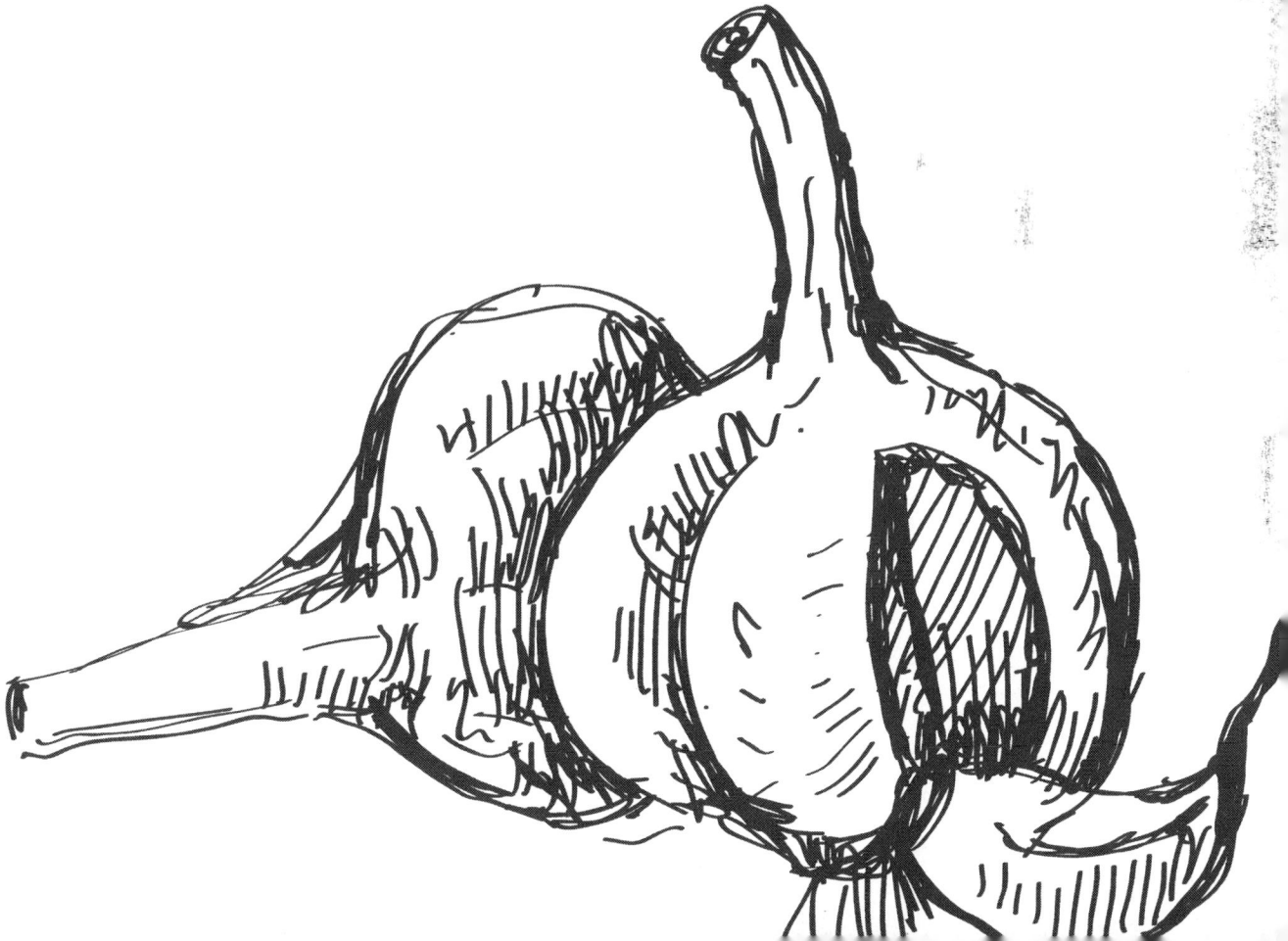

Table of Contents

Nasi Goreng 7

Indonesian Inspired Ketchup 8

Indonesian Fried Rice 9

Indonesian Classical Satay 10

Beef Satay 11

Indo-Chinese Spiced Rice 12

Indo-Chinese Chicken 13

Mie Goreng 14

Pisang Goreng 15

Kecap Manis Sedang 16

Satay Ayam 17

Skirt Steak 18

Prawn Nasi Goreng 19

Jemput Jumput 20

Chicken & Broccoli 21

Indo-Chinese Sate 22

Telur Balado 23

Ayam Masak Merah 24

Cap Cai 25

A Southeast Asian Sandwich 26

Shrimp Soup 27

Beef Pho 28

A Chicken & Curry Soup from Southeast Asia 29

Chicken Curry I 30

Chicken Curry II 31

Corned Beef Waffles 32

Mango Bread 33

Corn and Cashew Hummus 34

Toasti 35

Banana Waffles 36

Seaweed Soup 37

Eggs Kimchi 38

Kimchee Jigeh 39

The Easiest Fruit Pie 40

Beef Stir-Fry 41

Tofu Mushroom Soup 42

Udon Soup 43

Shrimp Soup 44

Spinach Ramen Pasta Salad 45

Ramen Frittata 46

Chicken Ramen Stir-Fry 47

Peanut Pasta Ramen Noodles 48

Chestnut & Peppers Ramen Salad 49

Authentic Fried Rice II 50

Pepper Steak 51

Ginger Chicken 52

Authentic Fried Rice III 53

Sweet and Sour Eggplant 54

Braised Ribs 55

Asian Pancakes 56

Sesame Lemon Shrimp 57

Savory and Sweet Omelet 58

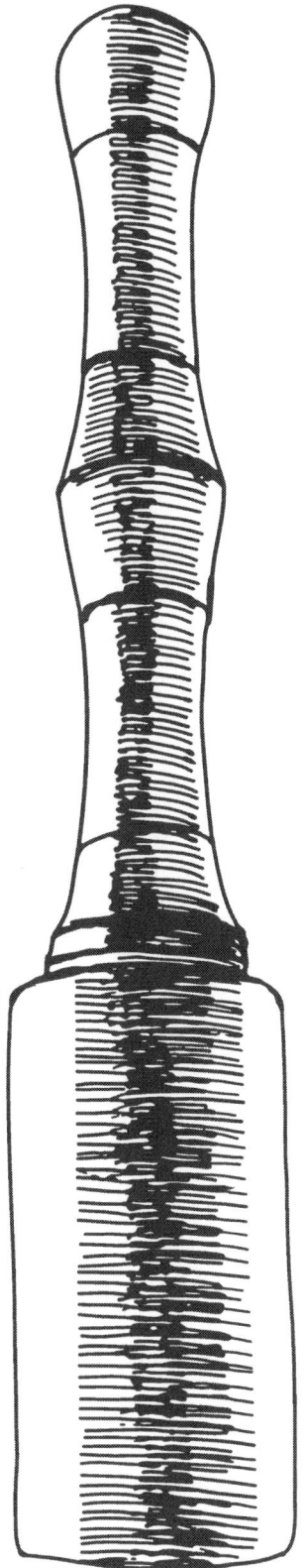

Noodles Curry Soup 59

Vanilla Crusted Shrimp 60

Nori Noodles Soup 61

Honey Chili and Peanut Noodles 62

Maggie's Easy Coconut Soup 63

Peanut, Jalapeno, and Cucumber Salad 64

Catalina's Spicy Wontons 65

Manitoba Maple Wontons 66

Silver Dragon Wonton Soup 67

Artisanal Wonton Tins 68

How to Make Wonton Wraps 69

Nasi Goreng (Chicken Fried Rice Dish with Sauce)

Prep Time: 15 mins
Total Time: 50 mins

Servings per Recipe: 6

Calories	430 kcal
Carbohydrates	51.5 g
Cholesterol	101 mg
Fat	13.8 g
Protein	24.3 g
Sodium	491 mg

Ingredients

12 ounces long grain white rice
3 cups water
salt to taste
2 tbsps sunflower seed oil
1 pound skinless, boneless chicken breast halves
2 cloves garlic, coarsely chopped
1 fresh red chile pepper, seeded and chopped
1 tbsp curry paste

1 bunch green onions, thinly sliced
2 tbsps soy sauce, or more to taste
1 tsp sunflower seed oil
2 eggs
2 ounces roasted peanuts, coarsely chopped
1/4 cup chopped fresh cilantro

Directions

1. Bring a mixture of rice, water and salt to boil in a pan before turning down the heat to low and cooking for another 25 minutes to get the rice tender.
2. Cook chicken, garlic and red chili pepper for about seven minutes before adding curry paste, cooked rice and green onion into it and cooking for another five minutes, while adding soy sauce at the end.
3. Put the rice mixture aside; cook egg in the in a pot and when finished, mix it with the rice very thoroughly.
4. Garnish with peanuts and cilantro before serving.

INDONESIAN INSPIRED
Ketchup

Prep Time: 5 mins
Total Time: 20 mins

Servings per Recipe: 3
Calories	31 kcal
Carbohydrates	7.4 g
Cholesterol	< 1 mg
Fat	0 g
Protein	0.5 g
Sodium	479 mg

Ingredients

1 1/4 cups soy sauce
1 cup molasses (such as Grandma's®)
2 tbsps brown sugar

1 cube chicken bouillon (such as Knorr®)

Directions

1. Mix all the ingredients mentioned above in a saucepan and cook it over low heat until you see that a slow boil is reached.
2. Turn the heat off and cool it down.
3. Store this in an airtight container and in a refrigerator.

Indonesian
Fried Rice

Prep Time: 25 mins
Total Time: 40 mins

Servings per Recipe: 4
Calories	215 kcal
Carbohydrates	26.7 g
Cholesterol	186 mg
Fat	7.7 g
Protein	10 g
Sodium	1033 mg

Ingredients

1/2 cup uncooked long grain white rice
1 cup water
2 tsps sesame oil
1 small onion, chopped
2 cloves garlic, minced
1 green chile pepper, chopped
1 small carrot, sliced
1 stalk celery, sliced

2 tbsps kecap manis
2 tbsps tomato sauce
2 tbsps soy sauce
1/4 cucumber, sliced
4 eggs

Directions

1. Bring a mixture of rice and water to boil before turning down the heat to low and cooking for 20 minutes.
2. Cook onion, green chili and garlic in hot oil for a few minutes before adding carrot, rice, tomato sauce, celery, soy sauce and kecap manis, and cooking for another few minutes.
3. Transfer this to a bowl, while garnishing with cucumber slices.
4. Cook eggs in the pan and when done, put them over rice and vegetables.

INDONESIAN
Classical Satay

Prep Time: 25 mins
Total Time: 1 hr

Servings per Recipe: 6	
Calories	329 kcal
Carbohydrates	11.8 g
Cholesterol	67 mg
Fat	18.2 g
Protein	30.8 g
Sodium	957 mg

Ingredients

3 tbsps soy sauce
3 tbsps tomato sauce
1 tbsp peanut oil
2 cloves garlic, peeled and minced
1 pinch ground black pepper
1 pinch ground cumin
6 skinless, boneless chicken breast halves - cubed
1 tbsp vegetable oil
1/4 cup minced onion

1 clove garlic, peeled and minced
1 cup water
1/2 cup chunky peanut butter
2 tbsps soy sauce
2 tbsps white sugar
1 tbsp lemon juice
skewers

Directions

1. At first you need to set a grill or grilling plate to high heat and put some oil before starting anything else.
2. Coat chicken with a mixture of soy sauce, cumin, tomato sauce, black pepper, peanut oil and garlic, and refrigerate it for at least 15 minutes.
3. Cook onion and garlic in hot oil until brown before adding water, sugar, peanut butter and soy sauce into it. Add lemon juice after removing from heat.
4. Thread all the chicken pieces into skewers
5. Cook this on the preheated grill for about 5 minutes each side or until tender.
6. Serve this with peanut sauce.
7. NOTE: If using a grilling plate please adjust the cooking time of the meat, to make sure that everything is cooked fully through.
8. NOTE: For peanut sauce recipe please see recipe for Satay Ayam.
9. NOTE: You will find that a few of these recipes call for a grill. Real Southeast Asian food is cooked street-style over an open flame, outside. For maximum authenticity use a grill.

Beef Satay

🥣 Prep Time: 30 mins
🕐 Total Time: 6 hrs 40 mins

Servings per Recipe: 4
Calories	683 kcal
Carbohydrates	22.1 g
Cholesterol	156 mg
Fat	49.7 g
Protein	41.6 g
Sodium	2332 mg

Ingredients

2 cloves garlic
1/2 cup chopped green onions
1 tbsp chopped fresh ginger root
1 cup roasted, salted Spanish peanuts
2 tbsps lemon juice
2 tbsps honey
1/2 cup soy sauce
2 tsps crushed coriander seed

1 tsp red pepper flakes
1/2 cup chicken broth
1/2 cup melted butter
1 1/2 pounds beef tenderloin, cut into 1 inch cubes
skewers

Directions

1. At first you need to set a grill or grilling plate to medium heat and put some oil before starting anything else.
2. Blend garlic, ginger, soy sauce, peanuts, lemon juice, honey, green onions, coriander, and red pepper flakes in a blender until you see that a smoothness is achieved.
3. Coat beef cubes with this mixture by placing everything in a plastic bag and refrigerating for at least six hours.
4. Thread beef cubes taken out from the bag onto skewers and boil the remaining marinade for about 5 minutes
5. Cook this on the preheated grill for about 15 minutes each side or until tender, while brushing frequently with the cooked marinade.
6. Serve with the remaining marinade.
7. NOTE: If using a grilling plate please adjust the cooking time of the meat, to make sure that everything is cooked fully through.

INDO-CHINESE
Spiced Rice

Prep Time: 10 mins
Total Time: 35 mins

Servings per Recipe: 8
Calories	226 kcal
Carbohydrates	39.8 g
Cholesterol	0 mg
Fat	5.5 g
Protein	3.7 g
Sodium	4 mg

Ingredients

3 tbsps vegetable oil
1 large onion, chopped
2 jalapeno peppers, seeded and minced
2 cloves garlic, crushed
1 tsp ground turmeric
1/2 tsp ground cinnamon
2 cups uncooked long-grain white rice

2 (14.5 ounce) cans chicken broth
1 cup water
1 bay leaf
2 green onions, chopped

Directions

1. Cook onion, garlic and jalapeno peppers for about eight minutes before adding turmeric and cooking for two more minutes.
2. Now add chicken broth, bay leaf and water, and cook all this for about 20 minutes after bringing this mixture to boil.
3. Turn the heat off and let it stand as it is for about five minutes.
4. Sprinkle some green onion over it before serving.

Indo-Chinese
Chicken

🥣 Prep Time: 15 mins
🕐 Total Time: 45 mins

Servings per Recipe: 4
Calories	530 kcal
Carbohydrates	58.1 g
Cholesterol	59 mg
Fat	18.6 g
Protein	35.4 g
Sodium	322 mg

Ingredients

1 cup uncooked long grain white rice
2 cups water
1 pound fresh green beans, trimmed and snapped
2 tsps olive oil
1 pound skinless, boneless chicken breast halves - cut into chunks
3/4 cup low-sodium chicken broth

1/3 cup smooth peanut butter
2 tsps honey
1 tbsp low sodium soy sauce
1 tsp red chile paste
2 tbsps lemon juice
3 green onions, thinly sliced
2 tbsps chopped peanuts(optional)

Directions

1. Bring a mixture of rice and water to boil before turning down the heat to low and cooking for 20 minutes.
2. Put green beans in a steamer basket over boiling water and steam it for about ten minutes or until you find that it is tender.
3. Cook chicken in hot oil for about five minutes on each side.
4. Combine chicken broth, honey, soy sauce, peanut butter, chile paste and lemon juice in a pan, and cook it for about five minutes before adding green beans.
5. Serve this over rice and garnish with green onions and peanuts.

MIE GORENG
(Indonesian Fried Noodles)

Prep Time: 15 mins
Total Time: 40 mins

Servings per Recipe: 6
Calories	356 kcal
Carbohydrates	34 g
Cholesterol	43 mg
Fat	14.3 g
Protein	22.7 g
Sodium	1824 mg

Ingredients

3 (3 ounce) packages ramen noodles (without flavor packets)
1 tbsp vegetable oil
1 pound skinless, boneless chicken breast halves, cut into strips
1 tsp olive oil
1 tsp garlic salt
1 pinch ground black pepper, or to taste
1 tbsp vegetable oil
1/2 cup chopped shallots
5 cloves garlic, chopped
1 cup shredded cabbage

1 cup shredded carrots
1 cup broccoli florets
1 cup sliced fresh mushrooms
1/4 cup soy sauce
1/4 cup sweet soy sauce (Indonesian kecap manis)
1/4 cup oyster sauce
salt and pepper to taste

Directions

1. Cook noodles in boiling water for about 3 minutes before running it through cold water to stop the process of cooking and draining all the water.
2. Coat chicken strips with olive oil, black pepper and garlic salt before cooking it in hot oil for about 5 minutes or until you see that the chicken is no longer pink.
3. Now add garlic and shallots, and cook them until you see that they are turning brown.
4. Now add all the vegetables into the pan and cook it for another five minutes or until you see that the vegetables are tender.
5. Add the mixture of noodles, soy sauce, oyster sauce and sweet soy sauce into the pan containing chicken and vegetables.
6. Sprinkle some salt and pepper before serving.
7. Enjoy.

Pisang Goreng
(Indonesian Banana Fritters I)

Prep Time: 5 mins
Total Time: 20 mins

Servings per Recipe: 4
Calories	489 kcal
Carbohydrates	73.2 g
Cholesterol	64 mg
Fat	19.5 g
Protein	8.3 g
Sodium	73 mg

Ingredients

1 1/4 cups all-purpose flour
2 tbsps granulated sugar
1/4 tbsp vanilla powder
1/2 cup milk
1 egg
2 tbsps butter, melted

1 tsp rum flavoring
4 ripe bananas, sliced
2 cups oil for frying

Directions

1. Mix flour, vanilla powder and sugar before making a space in the center and adding milk, melted butter, egg and rum flavoring.
2. Combine it thoroughly before adding banana slices.
3. Fry this banana mixture in hot oil for about 15 minutes or until golden brown.
4. Remove these bananas from the oil and drain it well with the help of paper towels.
5. Serve.

KECAP
Manis Sedang (Indo-Chinese Soy Sauce)

Prep Time: 5 mins
Total Time: 20 mins

Servings per Recipe: 12
Calories	54 kcal
Carbohydrates	13.1 g
Cholesterol	0 mg
Fat	0 g
Protein	0.9 g
Sodium	806 mg

Ingredients

2/3 cup soy sauce
1 cup water
2/3 cup brown sugar

8 bay leaves

Directions

1. In a mixture of sugar, water and soy sauce in a saucepan, put bay leaves and bring all this to a boil.
2. Now turn down the heat to medium and cook it for another 30 minutes.
3. Let cool.
4. NOTE: This recipe is very important for multiple Indonesian and Indo-Chinese dishes mentioned throughout this cookbook.

Satay Ayam (Indo chicken with Peanut Sauce)

Prep Time: 10 mins
Total Time: 40 mins

Servings per Recipe: 4
Calories	326 kcal
Carbohydrates	8.9 g
Cholesterol	70 mg
Fat	21.8 g
Protein	24.9 g
Sodium	1339 mg

Ingredients

1 pound chicken thighs, cut into 1/2-inch pieces
3/4 tsp salt
1 pinch ground white pepper
1 tbsp sunflower seed oil
24 wooden skewers
Peanut Sauce:
1 cup water
5 tbsps peanut butter
2 tbsps kecap manis (sweet soy sauce)
1 tbsp brown sugar
2 cloves garlic, minced
1/2 tsp salt
1 tbsp lime juice

Directions

1. Coat chicken thighs with ¾ tsp salt, sunflower seed oil and white pepper before refrigerating it for at least two hours.
2. Bring a mixture of water, salt, peanut butter, kecap manis, garlic and brown sugar to boil before removing it from heat and adding some lime juice to make peanut sauce.
3. Thread these chicken thighs onto skewers, while saving some marinade for later use.
4. Cook these chicken thighs on a preheated grill for about 2 minutes each side or until tender.
5. Serve this with peanut sauce.
6. NOTE: You can use a grilling plate as well for this recipe, just increase the cooking time of the meat. Use of a grill is preferred.

SKIRT
Steak

Prep Time: 15 mins
Total Time: 35 mins

Servings per Recipe: 6
Calories	437 kcal
Carbohydrates	46.2 g
Cholesterol	27 mg
Fat	4.8 g
Protein	22.5 g
Sodium	6517 mg

Ingredients

1 1/2 cups sweet soy sauce (Indonesian kecap manis)
1 cup sake
1 cup pineapple juice
1 cup mirin
1/2 cup reduced-sodium soy sauce
1/4 bunch fresh cilantro, chopped
1 tbsp white sugar

1 tbsp minced fresh ginger root
1 tbsp minced garlic
1 tbsp chopped scallions (green onions)
1 tbsp chili paste(optional)
1 (1 pound) skirt steak

Directions

1. At first you need to set grill or grilling plate to medium heat and put some oil before starting anything else.
2. Mix sweet soy sauce (kecap manis), scallions, sake, mirin, reduced-sodium soy sauce, cilantro, pineapple juice, sugar, ginger, garlic, and chili paste in large sized glass bowl before coating skirt steak with this mixture.
3. Wrap it up with a plastic bag and marinate it for at least three hours.
4. Remove every piece of meat from the marinade and cook this marinade in a saucepan for about 10 minutes over medium heat.
5. Cook meat on the preheated grill for about 8 minutes each side or until tender.
6. Serve it with the cooked marinade.
7. NOTE: If using a grilling plate please adjust the cooking time of the meat, to make sure that everything is cooked fully through.

Prawn
Nasi Goreng (Fried Rice and Shrimp In Sauce)

🥣 Prep Time: 20 mins
🕐 Total Time: 30 mins

Servings per Recipe: 2

Calories	664 kcal
Carbohydrates	67.7 g
Cholesterol	500 mg
Fat	25.5 g
Protein	41 g
Sodium	1497 mg

Ingredients

2 tbsps vegetable oil, divided
3 eggs, beaten
2 tbsps dark soy sauce
2 tbsps ketchup
1 tbsp brown sugar
1 tsp toasted sesame oil
1 tsp sweet chili sauce
1 zucchini, chopped

1 carrot, chopped
8 green onions, sliced
1 clove garlic, crushed
2 cups cooked rice
1/2 pound cooked prawns
2 tbsps fresh chives, chopped

Directions

1. Cook egg in hot oil for about 30 seconds each side and cut it into smaller pieces after letting it cool down.
2. Mix soy sauce, brown sugar, sesame oil, ketchup and chili sauce in a bowl, and set it aside for later use.
3. Cook zucchini, green onions and carrot in hot oil for about three minutes before adding garlic, sauce mixture, rice and prawns.
4. Turn the heat off and serve it by topping with eggs and sliced chives.

JEMPUT JUMPUT
(Indo Banana Fritters II)

Prep Time: 10 mins
Total Time: 25 mins

Servings per Recipe: 18
Calories   491 kcal
Carbohydrates   14.4 g
Cholesterol   0 mg
Fat   49.1 g
Protein   0.9 g
Sodium   49 mg

Ingredients

5/8 cup all-purpose flour
1 pinch salt
1 tsp baking powder
6 ripe bananas

3 tbsps white sugar
oil for frying

Directions

1. Add a mixture of baking powder, flour and salt slowly into mashed bananas and sugar, while stirring continuously.
2. Drop this mixture with help of a spoon into hot oil and cook for about 8 minutes, while turning only once.
3. Serve after draining with paper towels.

Chicken
& Broccoli

Prep Time: 10 mins
Total Time: 35 mins

Servings per Recipe: 6
Calories	170 kcal
Carbohydrates	9.8 g
Cholesterol	33 mg
Fat	7.9 g
Protein	16.2 g
Sodium	418 mg

Ingredients

12 ounces boneless, skinless chicken breast halves, cut into bite-sized pieces
1 tbsp oyster sauce
2 tbsps dark soy sauce
3 tbsps vegetable oil
2 cloves garlic, chopped
1 large onion, cut into rings
1/2 cup water

1 tsp ground black pepper
1 tsp white sugar
1/2 medium head bok choy, chopped
1 small head broccoli, chopped
1 tbsp cornstarch, mixed with equal parts water

Directions

1. Mix chicken, soy sauce and oyster sauce in large bowl and set it aside for later use.
2. Cook garlic and onion in hot oil for about three minutes before adding chicken mixture and cooking it for another ten minutes.
3. Now add water, sugar, broccoli, pepper and bok choy, and cook it for another ten minutes.
4. In the end, add cornstarch mixture and cook it for another 5 minutes to get the sauce thick.
5. Enjoy.

INDO-CHINESE
Sate
(Meat Kabobs)

Prep Time: 15 mins
Total Time: 2 hrs 20 mins

Servings per Recipe: 4	
Calories	200 kcal
Carbohydrates	6.5 g
Cholesterol	69 mg
Fat	5.4 g
Protein	25.1 g
Sodium	419 mg

Ingredients

1 onion, chopped
1 clove garlic, minced
1 1/2 tbsps kecap manis
1 tsp ground coriander
1 tsp ground cumin
1 tsp sambal oelek (sriracha sauce)
1/2 cup red wine
1 1/2 tbsps water

1 lemon grass, bruised, and cut into 1 inch pieces
1 pound sirloin steak, cut into 1-inch cubes

Directions

1. At first you need to set a grill or grilling plate to medium heat and put some oil before starting anything else.
2. Blend onion, garlic, coriander, cumin, kecap manis, sambal oelek, red wine and water in a blender until smooth before adding lemon grass and coating beef with this marinade.
3. Wrap it up with a plastic bag and refrigerate it for at least two hours.
4. Thread these beef pieces onto the skewers.
5. Cook this on the preheated grill for about 5 minutes each side or until tender.
6. NOTE: If using a grilling plate please adjust the cooking time of the meat, to make sure that everything is cooked fully through.

Telur Balado
(Spicy Indonesian Eggs)

🥘 Prep Time: 15 mins
🕐 Total Time: 35 mins

Servings per Recipe: 6
Calories   237 kcal
Carbohydrates   13.1 g
Cholesterol   201 mg
Fat   17.3 g
Protein   9.1 g
Sodium   115 mg

Ingredients

1 cup vegetable oil for frying
6 hard-boiled eggs, shells removed
6 red chili peppers, seeded and chopped
4 cloves garlic
4 medium shallots
2 tomatoes, quartered
1 tsp shrimp paste
1 1/2 tbsps peanut oil

1 tbsp vegetable oil
1 tsp white vinegar
1 tsp white sugar
salt and pepper to taste

Directions

1. Deep fry eggs in a pan for about seven minutes over medium heat or until golden brown in color.
2. Put chili peppers, shallots, garlic, tomatoes, and shrimp in a blender until you see that the required smoothness is achieved.
3. Cook chili pepper mixture in hot oil before adding vinegar, pepper, sugar, fried eggs and salt into a mixture.
4. Turn down the heat to medium and cook it for about 5 minutes, while turning it frequently.
5. Serve.

AYAM
Masak Merah (Spicy Tomato Chicken)

Prep Time: 20 mins
Total Time: 55 mins

Servings per Recipe: 4
Calories	462 kcal
Carbohydrates	15.4 g
Cholesterol	92 mg
Fat	29.7 g
Protein	33.6 g
Sodium	183 mg

Ingredients

1 (3 pound) whole chicken, cut into 8 pieces
1 tsp ground turmeric
salt to taste
1/4 cup dried red chili peppers
3 fresh red chili pepper, finely chopped
4 cloves garlic, minced
1 red onion, chopped
1 (3/4 inch thick) slice fresh ginger root
2 tbsps sunflower seed oil
1 cinnamon stick
2 whole star anise pods

5 whole cloves
5 cardamom seeds
2 tomatoes, sliced
2 tbsps ketchup
1 tsp white sugar, or to taste
1/2 cup water

Directions

1. Coat chicken with turmeric powder and salt, and set it aside for later use.
2. Put dried red chili peppers in hot water until you see that it is soft.
3. Put softened dried chili, garlic, fresh red chili peppers, onion, and ginger in a blender and blend it until you get a paste.
4. Cook chicken in hot oil until you see that it is golden from all sides and set it aside.
5. Now cook chili paste, cinnamon, cardamom seeds, star anise, and cloves in the same pan for few minutes before adding chicken and water into it.
6. Add tomatoes, sugar and ketchup, and bring all this to a boil before turning down the heat to medium and cooking for another 15 minutes.
7. Serve.

Cap Cai
(Indo-Chinese Shrimp Veggie Salad)

Prep Time: 20 mins
Total Time: 45 mins

Servings per Recipe: 4	
Calories	250 kcal
Carbohydrates	18.7 g
Cholesterol	106 mg
Fat	11.9 g
Protein	18.9 g
Sodium	819 mg

Ingredients

3 tbsps vegetable oil
4 cloves garlic, minced
1 onion, thinly sliced
10 ounces peeled and deveined medium shrimp (30-40 per pound)
1 head bok choy, chopped
1 1/2 cups chopped broccoli
1 1/2 cups chopped cauliflower
1 large carrot, thinly sliced at an angle
3 green onions, chopped

2/3 cup water
2 tbsps cornstarch
2 tbsps fish sauce
2 tbsps oyster sauce
1 tsp white sugar
1/2 tsp ground black pepper
salt to taste

Directions

1. Cook onion and garlic in hot oil for about five minutes before adding shrimp, broccoli, cauliflower, bok choy, carrot, water and green onion, and cook this for about 15 minutes or until you see that all the vegetables are tender.
2. Add a mixture of fish sauce and cornstarch, to the cap cai and also some oyster sauce, pepper and sugar.
3. Mix it thoroughly and add some salt according to your taste before serving.

A SOUTHEAST ASIAN
Sandwich

Prep Time: 10 mins
Total Time: 15 mins

Servings per Recipe: 4

Calories	627 kcal
Carbohydrates	72.1 g
Cholesterol	124 mg
Fat	12.1 g
Protein	55.3 g
Sodium	1005 mg

Ingredients

4 boneless beef loin chops, cut 1/4 inch thick
4 (7 inch) French bread baguettes, split lengthwise
4 tsps mayonnaise, or to taste
1 ounce chile sauce with garlic (sriracha sauce)
1/4 cup fresh lime juice

1 small red onion, sliced into rings
1 medium cucumber, peeled and sliced lengthwise
2 tbsps chopped fresh cilantro
salt and pepper to taste

Directions

1. Put beef chops in a broiling pan and cook it for about 5 minutes or until you see that it is brown from each side.
2. Put mayonnaise evenly on French rolls and also put one beef chop on each roll.
3. Put chili sauce on the meat and add some lime juice, while topping it with onion, pepper, cucumber, salt and cilantro.
4. Add some more lime juice just before serving.

Shrimp
Soup

Prep Time: 15 mins
Total Time: 40 mins

Servings per Recipe: 6
Calories	212 kcal
Carbohydrates	28.6 g
Cholesterol	52 mg
Fat	4.7 g
Protein	14.4 g
Sodium	1156 mg

Ingredients

1 tbsp vegetable oil
2 tsps minced fresh garlic
2 tsps minced fresh ginger root
1 (10 ounce) package frozen chopped spinach, thawed and drained
salt and black pepper to taste
2 quarts chicken stock
1 cup shrimp stock

1 tsp hot pepper sauce(optional)
1 tsp hoisin sauce(optional)
20 peeled and deveined medium shrimp
1 (6.75 ounce) package long rice noodles (rice vermicelli)
2 green onions, chopped(optional)

Directions

1. Cook garlic and ginger for about one minute before adding spinach, pepper and salt, and cooking it for 3 more minutes to get the spinach tender.
2. Add chicken stock, hoisin sauce, shrimp stock and hot pepper sauce, and cook this for a few more minutes.
3. In the end, add noodles and shrimp into it, and cook it for 4 minutes before adding green onions cooking it for another five minutes.
4. Add salt and pepper according to your taste before serving.
5. Enjoy.

BEEF
Pho

🥘 Prep Time: 10 mins
🕐 Total Time: 1 hr 30 mins

Servings per Recipe: 6	
Calories	528 kcal
Carbohydrates	73.1 g
Cholesterol	51 mg
Fat	13.6 g
Protein	27.1 g
Sodium	2844 mg

Ingredients

4 quarts beef broth
1 large onion, sliced into rings
6 slices fresh ginger root
1 lemon grass
1 cinnamon stick
1 tsp whole black peppercorns
1 pound sirloin tip, cut into thin slices
1/2 pound bean sprouts
1 cup fresh basil leaves
1 cup fresh mint leaves

1 cup loosely packed cilantro leaves
3 fresh jalapeno peppers, sliced into rings
2 limes, cut into wedges
2 (8 ounce) packages dried rice noodles
1/2 tbsp hoisin sauce
1 dash hot pepper sauce
3 tbsps fish sauce

Directions

1. Bring the mixture of broth, onion, lemon grass, cinnamon, ginger and peppercorns to boil before turning down the heat to low and cooking it for about one hour.
2. Place bean sprouts, basil, cilantro, chilies, mint and lime on a platter very neatly.
3. Place noodles in hot water for about 15 minutes before placing it in six different bowls evenly.
4. Put raw beef over it before pouring in hot broth.
5. Serve it with the platter and sauces.

A Chicken
& Curry Soup from Southeast Asia

🥣 Prep Time: 30 mins

🕐 Total Time: 2 hrs 30 mins

Servings per Recipe: 8

Calories	512 kcal
Carbohydrates	40.6 g
Cholesterol	75 mg
Fat	26.8 g
Protein	29.8 g
Sodium	374 mg

Ingredients

2 tbsps vegetable oil

1 (3 pound) whole chicken, skin removed and cut into pieces

1 onion, cut into chunks

2 shallots, thinly sliced

2 cloves garlic, chopped

1/8 cup thinly sliced fresh ginger root

1 stalk lemon grass, cut into 2 inch pieces

4 tbsps curry powder

1 green bell pepper, cut into 1 inch pieces

2 carrots, sliced diagonally

1 quart chicken broth

1 quart water

2 tbsps fish sauce

2 kaffir lime leaves

1 bay leaf

2 tsps red pepper flakes

8 small potatoes, quartered

1 (14 ounce) can coconut milk

1 bunch fresh cilantro

Directions

1. Cook onion and chicken in hot oil until you see that onions are soft and then set it aside for later use.

2. Cook shallots in the same pan for one minute before adding garlic, lemon grass, ginger and curry powder, and cooking it for another five minutes.

3. Add pepper and carrots before stirring in chicken, onion, fish sauce, chicken broth and water.

4. Also add lime leaves, red pepper flakes and bay leaf before bringing all this to boil and adding potatoes.

5. Add coconut milk and cook it for 60 minutes after turning down the heat to low.

6. Garnish with a sprig of fresh cilantro.

7. Serve.

CHICKEN
Curry I

Prep Time: 15 mins
Total Time: 55 mins

Servings per Recipe: 6

Calories	500 kcal
Carbohydrates	22.1 g
Cholesterol	58 mg
Fat	36.1 g
Protein	25.8 g
Sodium	437 mg

Ingredients

1 tbsp olive oil
3 tbsps Thai yellow curry paste (such as Mae Ploy®)
1 pound cooked skinless, boneless chicken breast, cut into bite-size pieces
2 (14 ounce) cans coconut milk
1 cup chicken stock

1 yellow onion, chopped
3 small red potatoes, cut into cubes, or as needed
3 red Thai chili peppers, chopped with seeds, or more to taste
1 tsp fish sauce

Directions

1. Mix curry paste in hot oil before adding chicken and coating it well.
2. Add 1 can coconut milk and cook it for five minutes before adding the rest of the coconut milk, onion, potatoes, chicken stock and chili peppers into it and bringing all this to boil.
3. Turn the heat down to low and cook for 25 minutes or until the potatoes are tender.
4. Add fish sauce into before serving.
5. Enjoy.

Chicken Curry II

🥣 Prep Time: 15 mins
🕐 Total Time: 35 mins

Servings per Recipe: 4
Calories   621 kcal
Carbohydrates   86.7 g
Cholesterol   91 mg
Fat   19.4 g
Protein   35.2 g
Sodium   316 mg

Ingredients

1 tbsp canola oil
2 tbsps green curry paste
1 pound boneless skinless chicken breasts, cut into bite-size pieces
1 small onion, thinly sliced
1 red pepper, cut into thin strips, then cut crosswise in half

1 green pepper, cut into thin strips, then cut crosswise in half
4 ounces cream cheese, cubed
1/4 cup milk
1/8 tsp white pepper
2 cups hot cooked long-grain white rice

Directions

1. Combine curry paste and hot oil before adding chicken and onions.
2. Cook this for about 8 minutes before adding green and red peppers, and cooking for another five minutes.
3. Now add cream cheese, white pepper and milk, and cook until you see that the cheese has melted.
4. Serve this on top of rice.
5. Enjoy.

CORNED BEEF
Waffles

Prep Time: 10 mins
Total Time: 20 mins

Servings per Recipe: 10

Calories	148 kcal
Carbohydrates	16 g
Cholesterol	54 mg
Fat	5.2 g
Protein	8.8 g
Sodium	268 mg

Ingredients

2 eggs
1 1/4 C. milk
2 tsps cooking oil
1 1/2 C. all-purpose flour
1 pinch salt

2 tsps baking powder
1/2 (12 ounce) can corned beef, broken into pieces

Directions

1. Heat a waffle iron before continuing.
2. Combine milk, oil and eggs in a bowl and in a separate bowl mix flour salt and baking powder.
3. Combine both mixtures and add beef.
4. Put this mixture into the preheated waffle iron and cook it until the waffles are golden in color.
5. Serve it with butter.

Mango Bread

Prep Time: 20 mins
Total Time: 1 hr 20 mins

Servings per Recipe: 2
Calories	193 kcal
Carbohydrates	27.2 g
Cholesterol	19 mg
Fat	8.9 g
Protein	2.1 g
Sodium	192 mg

Ingredients

2 C. all-purpose flour
2 tsps ground cinnamon
2 tsps baking soda
1/2 tsp salt
1 1/4 C. white sugar
2 eggs

3/4 C. vegetable oil
2 1/2 C. mangos, peeled, seeded and chopped
1 tsp lemon juice
1/4 C. raisins

Directions

1. Mix all the dry ingredients mentioned above and then add eggs beaten in oil to this mixture.
2. Now add mangoes, raisins and lemon.
3. Pour this into two different pans and bake at 350 degrees F for 60 minutes.
4. Serve.

CORN
and Cashew Hummus

Prep Time: 5 mins
Total Time: 5 mins

Servings per Recipe: 3

Calories	270 kcal
Carbohydrates	28.6 g
Cholesterol	0 mg
Fat	16.5 g
Protein	7.8 g
Sodium	367 mg

Ingredients

two cups corn kernels, thawed if frozen
one cup cashews
one tsp. lemon juice, or more to taste
1/4 tsp. salt
1/4 tsp. onion powder

1/4 tsp. garlic powder

Directions

1. Place everything mentioned in a blender and blend it for about one minute.
2. Serve with rice.

Toasti

🥣 Prep Time: 10 mins
🕐 Total Time: 20 mins

Servings per Recipe: 1
Calories	431 kcal
Carbohydrates	30.9 g
Cholesterol	247 mg
Fat	29.8 g
Protein	11.2 g
Sodium	751 mg

Ingredients

half cup shredded cabbage
half carrot, shredded
one egg
half tsp. soy sauce

two tbsps. butter
two slices bread, toasted

Directions

1. Add egg and soy sauce into a mixture of cabbage and carrot, and mix thoroughly.
2. Cook the patty made from this vegetable mixture in hot butter for about three minutes each side.
3. Serve by placing contents between two slices of bread.

BANANA
Waffles

Prep Time: 10 mins
Total Time: 40 mins

Servings per Recipe: 4
Calories	241 kcal
Carbohydrates	47.3 g
Cholesterol	50 mg
Fat	2.5 g
Protein	8.3 g
Sodium	606 mg

Ingredients

one 1/4 cups all-purpose flour
three tsps. baking powder
half tsp. salt
one pinch ground nutmeg
one cup 2% milk

one egg
two ripe bananas, sliced

Directions

1. Combine nutmeg, baking powder, flour and salt and add milk and eggs.
2. Pour two tbsps. of batter over preheated waffle iron after spraying the iron with non-stick cooking spray.
3. Now place two slices of banana on the mixture pour another two tsps. of batter over these slices of banana.
4. Cook for about three minutes or until golden brown.
5. Serve.

Seaweed
Soup

Prep Time: 15 mins
Total Time: 45 mins

Servings per Recipe: 4

Calories	65 kcal
Carbohydrates	1 g
Cholesterol	17 mg
Fat	3.7 g
Protein	6.8 g
Sodium	940 mg

Ingredients

one (one ounce) package dried brown
seaweed
1/4 lb. beef top sirloin, minced
two tsps. sesame oil
one half tbsps. soy sauce

one tsp. salt, or to taste
6 cups water
one tsp. minced garlic

Directions

1. Cover seaweed with water to get them soft and cut them into two inch pieces.
2. Cook beef, half tbsp. of soy sauce and some salt for about one minute in a saucepan over medium heat.
3. Now add seaweed and the remaining soy sauce and cook for another minute while stirring continuously.
4. Bring to boil after adding two cups of water and add garlic and the remaining water.
5. Cook this for 20 minutes and add salt before serving.

EGGS
Kimchi

Prep Time: 5 mins
Total Time: 10 mins

Servings per Recipe: 4
Calories	208 kcal
Carbohydrates	3.5 g
Cholesterol	186 mg
Fat	18.8 g
Protein	7.5 g
Sodium	568 mg

Ingredients

two tbsps. vegetable oil

one cup kimchi, or to taste

two large eggs, beaten

Directions

1. Cook kimchi in hot oil over medium heat for about two minutes and add eggs, and cook for another three minutes to get the eggs tender.

2. Serve.

Kimchee Jigeh (Stew)

Prep Time: 5 mins
Total Time: 25 mins

Servings per Recipe: 4

Calories	303 kcal
Carbohydrates	10.6 g
Cholesterol	59 mg
Fat	24.1 g
Protein	13.7 g
Sodium	2064 mg

Ingredients

6 cups water
three cups napa cabbage Kim Chee, brine reserved
two cups cubed fully cooked luncheon meat (e.g. Spam)

three tbsps. chili powder
salt, to taste
ground black pepper, to taste

Directions

1. Take a large saucepan and combine water, kim chee, spam, pepper, chili powder, kim chee brine and salt.
2. Bring this mixture to boil and cook for about 20 minutes.
3. Serve.

THE EASIEST
Fruit Pie

Prep Time: 10 mins
Total Time: 50 mins

Servings per Recipe: 1
Calories   404 kcal
Carbohydrates   47.7 g
Cholesterol   67 mg
Fat   23.1 g
Protein   3.8 g
Sodium   243 mg

Ingredients

1 (9 inch) unbaked pie shell
2 eggs, beaten
1/3 cup butter, melted
1 cup white sugar
1 tsp vanilla extract
1 tbsp distilled white vinegar
1/2 cup chopped pecans

1/2 cup shredded coconut
1/2 cup raisins

Directions

1. Get your oven hot to 350 degrees.
2. Get a bowl. Mix together until even and smooth: vinegar, eggs, sugar and butter.
3. Mix in raisins, pecans, and coconut. Put everything in a pie crust.
4. Bake for 40 mins.
5. Enjoy.

Beef Stir-Fry

🥣 Prep Time: 30 mins
🕐 Total Time: 45 mins

Servings per Recipe: 8
Calories   290 kcal
Carbohydrates   26.4 g
Cholesterol   39 mg
Fat   7.6 g
Protein   26.4 g
Sodium   1271 mg

Ingredients

2 pounds boneless beef sirloin or beef top round steaks (3/4" thick)
3 tbsps cornstarch
1 (10.5 ounce) can Campbell's® Condensed Beef Broth
1/2 cup soy sauce
2 tbsps sugar
2 tbsps vegetable oil

4 cups sliced shiitake mushrooms
1 head Chinese cabbage (bok choy), thinly sliced
2 medium red peppers, cut into 2"-long strips
3 stalks celery, sliced
2 medium green onions, cut into 2" pieces
Hot cooked regular long-grain white rice

Directions

1. To start this recipe grab a knife and begin to cut your beef into some thin long strips.
2. Grab a medium sized bowl and combine the following ingredients: sugar, broth, soy, and cornstarch.
3. After combining the ingredients set them aside.
4. Get your wok hot over a high level of heat and add one 1 tbsp of oil to it.
5. Once your oil is hot combine the following ingredients in it: green onions, mushrooms, celery, cabbage, and peppers.
6. Fry these veggies down until you find that they are soft. Set aside.
7. Now grab your cornstarch mixture and put it in the pot. Stir-fry until you find that it has thickened.
8. Once thick, combine the cornstarch with your beef and veggies.
9. Fry until beef is cooked completely.
10. Let contents cool.
11. Enjoy.

TOFU
Mushroom Soup

Prep Time: 10 mins
Total Time: 20 mins

Servings per Recipe: 2
Calories	100 kcal
Carbohydrates	4.8 g
Cholesterol	3 mg
Fat	3.9 g
Protein	11 g
Sodium	1326 mg

Ingredients

3 cups prepared dashi stock
1/4 cup sliced shiitake mushrooms
1 tbsp miso paste
1 tbsp soy sauce

1/8 cup cubed soft tofu
1 green onion, diced

Directions

1. Get a saucepan. Add your stock, get it boiling. Once boiling add mushrooms and cook for 4 mins.
2. Get a bowl. Combine soy sauce and miso paste evenly. Mix this with your stock.
3. For 6 mins let broth cook. Add some diced green onion.
4. Enjoy.

Udon Soup

🍜 Prep Time: 15 mins
🕐 Total Time: 40 mins

Servings per Recipe: 4
Calories   548 kcal
Carbohydrates   53.4 g
Cholesterol   206 mg
Fat   17.2 g
Protein   42.2 g
Sodium   2491 mg

Ingredients

6 cups prepared dashi stock
1/4 pound chicken, cut into chunks
2 carrots, diced
1/3 cup soy sauce
3 tbsps mirin
1/2 tsp white sugar
1/3 tsp salt

2 (12 ounce) packages firm tofu, cubed
1/3 pound shiitake mushrooms, sliced
5 ribs and leaves of bok choy, diced
1 (9 ounce) package fresh udon noodles
4 eggs
2 leeks, diced

Directions

1. Get a sauce pan. Heat the following: salt, dashi stock, sugar, carrots, mirin, chicken, and soy sauce. Allow everything to lightly boil until your chicken is cooked fully (8 mins).
2. Mix in some bok choy, mushrooms, and tofu. Let everything continue simmering for 6 mins.
3. Add your noodles and cook for 5 more mins. Finally add leeks.
4. Take your eggs and crack them over the soup. Let the soup cook for 5 mins until eggs are done.
5. Enjoy.

SHRIMP
Soup

Prep Time: 15 mins
Total Time: 40 mins

Servings per Recipe: 6
Calories	212 kcal
Carbohydrates	28.6 g
Cholesterol	52 mg
Fat	4.7 g
Protein	14.4 g
Sodium	1156 mg

Ingredients

1 tbsp vegetable oil
2 tsps minced fresh garlic
2 tsps minced fresh ginger root
1 (10 ounce) package frozen chopped spinach, thawed and drained
salt and black pepper to taste
2 quarts chicken stock
1 cup shrimp stock
1 tsp hot pepper sauce(optional)

1 tsp hoisin sauce(optional)
20 peeled and deveined medium shrimp
1 (6.75 ounce) package long rice noodles (rice vermicelli)
2 green onions, chopped(optional)

Directions

1. Cook garlic and ginger for about one minute before adding spinach, pepper and salt, and cooking it for 3 more minutes to get the spinach tender.
2. Add chicken stock, hoisin sauce, shrimp stock and hot pepper sauce, and cook this for a few more minutes.
3. In the end, add noodles and shrimp into it, and cook it for 4 minutes before adding green onions cooking it for another five minutes.
4. Add salt and pepper according to your taste before serving.
5. Enjoy.

Spinach
Ramen Pasta Salad

Prep Time: 15 mins
Total Time: 25 mins

Servings per Recipe: 2

Calories	147 kcal
Carbohydrates	11 g
Cholesterol	17 mg
Fat	8.6 g
Protein	7.2 g
Sodium	177 mg

Ingredients

2 (3 ounce) packages chicken flavored ramen noodles
8 cups torn spinach leaves
2 cups cooked and cubed chicken
1 cup seedless red grapes, halved
1 cup sliced red bell peppers
1/2 cup chopped cashews
1/2 cup Gorgonzola cheese, crumbled
4 cloves garlic, minced
1 lemon, juiced

1/3 cup olive oil
1/4 cup light mayonnaise
1 red bell pepper, sliced
20 grape clusters, for garnish

Directions

1. Cook ramen noodles in boiling water for about 2 minutes and drain it with the help of colander.
2. Mix torn spinach leaves, halved grapes, blue cheese, cooked turkey or chicken, red pepper, cashews and ramen noodles very thorough in a large bowl.
3. In another bowl; whisk lemon juice, flavor packets, oil, garlic and mayonnaise very thoroughly.
4. Pour this dressing that you just prepared over the salad and garnish this salad with some red pepper rings and small grape clusters.
5. Serve.

RAMEN
Frittata

🥣 Prep Time: 5 mins
🕐 Total Time: 20 mins

Servings per Recipe: 4
Calories	339 kcal
Carbohydrates	28.8 g
Cholesterol	302 mg
Fat	15.7 g
Protein	20.3 g
Sodium	681 mg

Ingredients

2 (3 ounce) packages chicken flavored ramen noodles
6 eggs

2 tsps butter
1/2 cup shredded Cheddar cheese

Directions

1. Cook ramen noodles in boiling water for about 2 minutes and drain it with the help of colander.
2. Pour the mixture of eggs and content of seasoning packets over noodles before cooking this in hot butter for about seven minutes.
3. Turn it over after cutting it into four slices and brown both sides.
4. Put some cheese over the top before serving.

Chicken
Ramen Stir-Fry

Prep Time: 15 mins
Total Time: 30 mins

Servings per Recipe: 2
Calories	438 kcal
Carbohydrates	47.6 g
Cholesterol	65 mg
Fat	14.1 g
Protein	31.9 g
Sodium	1118 mg

Ingredients

1 1/2 cups hot water
1 (3 ounce) package Oriental-flavor ramen noodle soup mix
2 tsps vegetable oil, divided
8 ounces skinless, boneless chicken breast halves, cut into 2-inch strips
2 cups broccoli florets
1 cup sliced onion wedges
2 cloves garlic, minced
1 cup fresh bean sprouts

1/2 cup water
1/2 cup sliced water chestnuts
1 tsp soy sauce
1 tsp oyster sauce
1/4 tsp chili-garlic sauce (such as Sriracha®), or to taste
1 roma tomato, cut into wedges

Directions

1. Cook ramen noodles in boiling water for about 2 minutes and drain it with the help of colander.

2. Now cook chicken in hot oil for about 5 minutes and set it aside in a bowl.

3. In the same skillet; Cook broccoli, garlic and onion for about three minutes before adding noodles, water, oyster sauce, chili garlic sauce, water chestnuts, bean sprouts, soy sauce and seasoning from the ramen noodle package.

4. Cook all this for about 5 minutes before adding tomato wedges and cooking it for three more minutes.

PEANUT
Pasta Ramen Noodles

Prep Time: 15 mins
Total Time: 20 mins

Servings per Recipe: 4
Calories	613 kcal
Carbohydrates	62.5 g
Cholesterol	0 mg
Fat	35.9 g
Protein	13.5 g
Sodium	2224 mg

Ingredients

1/3 cup peanut butter
3 tbsps vegetable oil
3 tbsps vinegar
2 tbsps soy sauce
1 clove garlic, minced
1 tsp white sugar
1/4 tsp cayenne pepper, or to taste
4 (3 ounce) packages ramen noodle soup (seasoning packets reserved for another use)

1/2 small cucumber, peeled and cut into matchsticks
1 green onion, thinly sliced
1/4 cup chopped cilantro
2 tbsps chopped salted peanuts

Directions

1. Cook ramen noodles in boiling water for about 2 minutes and drain it with the help of colander
2. Pour the mixture of peanut butter, vegetable oil, garlic, vinegar, soy sauce, sugar, and cayenne over noodles in a bowl, and mix it very thoroughly.
3. Add cucumber and green onion into it.
4. Garnish all this with peanuts and cilantro before serving.

Chestnut & Peppers Ramen Salad

Prep Time: 15 mins
Total Time: 25 mins

Servings per Recipe: 12
Calories	249 kcal
Carbohydrates	23.7 g
Cholesterol	7 mg
Fat	15 g
Protein	5.3 g
Sodium	427 mg

Ingredients

4 (3 ounce) packages chicken flavored ramen noodles
1 cup diced celery
1 (8 ounce) can water chestnuts, drained and sliced
1/2 red onion, diced

1/2 green bell pepper, diced
4 ounces frozen green peas
1 cup mayonnaise

Directions

1. Cook noodles according to the direction of the packets and drain it with the help of colander.
2. Pour mixture of mayonnaise and ramen noodle seasoning mix over the mixture of noodles, peas, celery, bell pepper, water chestnuts and red onion before refrigerating for at least an hour.
3. Serve.

AUTHENTIC
Fried Rice II

Prep Time: 5 mins
Total Time: 15 mins

Servings per Recipe: 4	
Calories	255 kcal
Fat	10.2 g
Carbohydrates	25.9g
Protein	14.1 g
Cholesterol	83 mg
Sodium	516 mg

Ingredients

1 egg
1 tbsp water
1 tbsp butter
1 tbsp vegetable oil
1 onion, diced
2 C. cooked white rice, cold

2 tbsps soy sauce
1 tsp ground black pepper
1 C. cooked, diced chicken meat

Directions

1. Get a bowl, combine: water and whisked eggs.
2. Get some butter hot in a frying pan then pour in your eggs.
3. Let the eggs sit for 3 mins then remove the eggs and cut them into strips.
4. Now being to stir fry your onions, until they are soft, in the same pan, then add in the chicken, rice, pepper, and soy sauce.
5. Cook the mix, while stirring, for 7 mins then add in the eggs and continue cooking everything for 2 more mins.
6. Enjoy.

Pepper Steak

Prep Time: 15 mins
Total Time: 30 mins

Servings per Recipe: 5

Calories	312 kcal
Fat	15.4 g
Carbohydrates	17g
Protein	26.1 g
Cholesterol	69 mg
Sodium	972 mg

Ingredients

1 lb beef top sirloin steak
1/4 C. soy sauce
2 tbsps white sugar
2 tbsps cornstarch
1/2 tsp ground ginger
3 tbsps vegetable oil, divided
1 red onion, cut into 1-inch squares

1 green bell pepper, cut into 1-inch squares
2 tomatoes, cut into wedges

Directions

1. Cut your steak into strips.
2. Get a bowl, combine: ginger, soy sauce, cornstarch, and sugar.
3. Combine the mix until the sugar dissolves. Then add in your steak and coat the pieces.
4. Now get 1 tbsp of veggie oil hot in a wok and add in one third of the steak to the pot.
5. Stir fry everything for 5 mins then place the steak into a bowl.
6. Continue frying your steak in thirds and placing the meat in the same bowl
7. Once the steak is cooked add everything back into the pot and also add in your onions.
8. Stir fry the mix for 4 mins then add the green pepper.
9. Continue cooking everything for 3 more mins then add in the tomatoes and get them hot.
10. Enjoy.

GINGER
Chicken

Prep Time: 30 mins
Total Time: 1 hr

Servings per Recipe: 4
Calories   393 kcal
Fat   10.3 g
Carbohydrates   41.9 g
Protein   34.1 g
Cholesterol   69 mg
Sodium   772 mg

Ingredients

3 tbsps hoisin sauce
2 tbsps peanut butter
2 tsps brown sugar
3/4 tsp hot chili paste
1 tsp grated fresh ginger
3 tbsps rice wine vinegar
1 tbsp sesame oil
1 lb skinless, boneless chicken breast halves

16 (3.5 inch square) wonton wrappers, shredded
4 C. romaine lettuce - torn, washed and dried
2 C. shredded carrots
1 bunch green onions, diced
1/4 C. diced fresh cilantro

Directions

1. Get a bowl, combine: sesame oil, hoisin, vinegar, peanut butter, ginger, chili paste, and brown sugar.
2. Broil your chicken for 12 mins. Then cut it into strips.
3. Now set your oven to 350 degrees before doing anything else.
4. Coat a casserole dish with nonstick spray and layer your wonton wrappers in it.
5. Cook the wrappers for 22 mins in the oven then let them cool.
6. Get a 2nd big bowl, mix: cilantro, chicken, green onions, wontons, carrots, and lettuce.
7. Combine in the sesame oil mix with the chicken mix and toss the contents to evenly distribute the dressing.
8. Enjoy.

Authentic Fried Rice III

🥣 Prep Time: 25 mins

🕐 Total Time: 40 mins

Servings per Recipe: 7

Calories	425 kcal
Fat	9.5 g
Carbohydrates	47.5g
Protein	34.7 g
Cholesterol	134 mg
Sodium	1060 mg

Ingredients

1/2 tbsp sesame oil
1 onion
1 1/2 lbs cooked, cubed chicken meat
2 tbsps soy sauce
2 large carrots, diced
2 stalks celery, diced
1 large red bell pepper, diced

3/4 C. fresh pea pods, halved
1/2 large green bell pepper, diced
6 C. cooked white rice
2 eggs
1/3 C. soy sauce

Directions

1. Stir fry your onions until tender then add in 2 tbsps of soy sauce and continue cooking the mix for 7 mins.

2. Add in your bell peppers, carrots, pea pods, and celery.

3. Continue frying the mix for 7 more mins.

4. Now add the eggs and 1/3 C. of soy sauce to the mix and cook everything until the eggs are scrambled and everything is heated.

5. Enjoy.

SWEET
and Sour
Eggplant

Prep Time: 30 mins
Total Time: 35 mins

Servings per Recipe: 4

Calories	153 kcal
Fat	7.8 g
Carbohydrates	21.1g
Protein	3.4 g
Cholesterol	0 mg
Sodium	1507 mg

Ingredients

2 long Chinese eggplants, cubed
1 1/2 tbsps soy sauce
1 tbsp red wine vinegar
1 tbsp white sugar
1 green chile pepper, diced
1 tsp cornstarch

1/2 tsp chili oil, or to taste
2 tsps salt
2 tbsps vegetable oil

Directions

1. Get a bowl, combine: salt and eggplant pieces.
2. Submerge everything in water and let the veggies sit for 40 mins.
3. Now remove all the liquids and run the eggplant under some fresh water.
4. Get a 2nd bowl, combine: chili oil, soy sauce, cornstarch, wine vinegar, chili peppers, and sugar.
5. Now being to stir fry your eggplant in veggie oil for 7 mins then add in the chili oil mix.
6. Let the contents cook until the sauce becomes thick.
7. Stir everything a few times then serve.
8. Enjoy.

Braised Ribs

Prep Time: 5 mins
Total Time: 1 hr 20 mins

Servings per Recipe: 4
Calories	244 kcal
Fat	18.5 g
Carbohydrates	3.5g
Protein	15.2 g
Cholesterol	60 mg
Sodium	536 mg

Ingredients

1 lb beef spareribs, cut into 3 inch pieces
1 tbsp vegetable oil
1 (1 inch) piece fresh ginger root, sliced
5 green onions cut into 2-inch pieces
1/2 tsp ground cinnamon
2 C. water
1 1/2 tbsps soy sauce

1 tsp white sugar
1 tsp rice wine
1/4 tsp salt
1/4 tsp pepper

Directions

1. Boil your spareribs in water for 7 mins then remove all the liquid.
2. Now being to stir fry your cinnamon, green onions, and ginger in veggie oil until the mix becomes aromatic.
3. Now add the ribs and cook everything for 6 more mins before adding: rice wine, pepper, water, salt, sugar, and soy sauce.
4. Get this mix boiling then set the heat to low and place a lid on the pan.
5. Let the mix cook for 65 mins.
6. Enjoy.

ASIAN
Pancakes

Prep Time: 30 mins
Total Time: 1 hr 45 mins

Servings per Recipe: 4
Calories	366 kcal
Fat	14.3 g
Carbohydrates	51.8g
Protein	7.5 g
Cholesterol	0 mg
Sodium	1757 mg

Ingredients

2 C. all-purpose flour
1 tbsp salt, divided
3/4 C. boiling water
1/2 C. cold water, or as needed
vegetable oil, or as needed, divided

1 bunch green onions (scallions), minced

Directions

1. Get a bowl, combine: 1 tsp salt and flour.
2. Add the boiling water and continue stirring everything.
3. Add in your cold water slowly in tbsp increments and make a dough.
4. Knead the dough for 12 mins then place it in a bowl with a damp kitchen towel as a cover.
5. Let the dough sit for 50 mins.
6. Now break the dough into 4 pieces and shape each piece in a thin round.
7. Coat each piece of dough with veggie oil and top everything with 1/4 of the onions and half a tsp of salt.
8. Now shape the dough around the onions then form everything into a disk. Continue shaping the dough pieces in this manner. Once you have 4 disks let then sit for 20 mins.
9. Shape disk into a pancake and fry it for 4 mins each side.
10. Continue frying the rest of the dough.
11. Enjoy.

Sesame Lemon Shrimp

Prep Time: 20 mins
Total Time: 1 hr 20 mins

Servings per Recipe: 9
Calories   286 kcal
Fat   15.7 g
Carbohydrates   3.8g
Protein   31 g
Cholesterol   230 mg
Sodium   355 mg

Ingredients

3 lbs jumbo shrimp, peeled and deveined
1/2 C. olive oil
2 tsps sesame oil
1/4 C. lemon juice
1 onion, diced
2 cloves garlic, peeled
2 tbsps grated fresh ginger root

2 tbsps diced fresh cilantro leaves
1 tsp paprika
1/2 tsp salt
1/2 tsp ground black pepper
skewers

Directions

1. Get a blender and process the following: pepper, olive oil, salt, sesame oil, paprika, lemon juice, cilantro, onion, ginger, and garlic.
2. Set a little to the side for later.
3. Get a bowl, and mix: the wet blender contents and your shrimp.
4. Let it marinate in the fridge for 2 hrs. while covered.
5. Skewer your shrimp and cook them on a preheated grill or grilling plate for 3 to 4 mins per side.
6. While the shrimp cooks make sure you baste it with some of the marinade that was set aside.
7. Enjoy.

SAVORY
and Sweet Omelet

Prep Time: 10 mins
Total Time: 15 mins

Servings per Recipe: 1

Calories	82 kcal
Fat	5 g
Carbohydrates	2.9g
Protein	6.6 g
Cholesterol	186 mg
Sodium	369 mg

Ingredients

1 tbsp water
1 tsp soy sauce, or to taste
1/2 tsp white sugar

1 egg

Directions

1. Get a mixing bowl: Whisk in it the water, soy sauce, and sugar well. Stir in the egg and mix them again.
2. Place a large skillet over medium heat. Grease it with a cooking spray. Pour into it the egg mix and spread it in the pan.
3. Cook it for 4 min until it becomes golden brown from the sides. Serve it warm.
4. Enjoy.

Noodles
Curry Soup

Prep Time: 15 mins
Total Time: 40 mins

Servings per Recipe: 4

Calories	442 kcal
Fat	15.8 g
Carbohydrates	65.2g
Protein	9.2 g
Cholesterol	0 mg
Sodium	1854 mg

Ingredients

3 carrots, cut into bite-size pieces
1 small onion, cut into bite-size pieces
3 tbsp water
1/4 C. vegetable oil
1/2 C. all-purpose flour
2 tbsp all-purpose flour
2 tbsp red curry powder

5 C. hot vegetable stock
1/4 C. soy sauce
2 tsp maple syrup
8 oz udon noodles, or more to taste

Directions

1. Get a microwave proof bowl: Stir in it the water with carrot and onion. put on the lid and cook them on high for 4 min 30 sec.
2. Place a soup pot over medium heat. Heat the oil in it. Add to it 1/2 C. plus 2 tbsp flour and mix them to make a paste.
3. Add the curry with hot stock and cook them for 4 min while mixing all the time. Add the cooked onion and carrot with soy sauce, and maple syrup.
4. Cook the noodles according to the directions on the package until it becomes soft.
5. Cook the soup until it starts boiling. Stir in the noodles and serve your soup hot.
6. Enjoy.

VANILLA
Crusted Shrimp

Prep Time: 5 mins
Total Time: 2 hrs 15 mins

Servings per Recipe: 6	
Calories	920 kcal
Fat	81.4 g
Carbohydrates	35.8g
Protein	14.1 g
Cholesterol	117 mg
Sodium	225 mg

Ingredients

32 vanilla wafers, crushed
1 egg, beaten
3/4 C. water
1/3 C. apricot nectar
2 tsp cornstarch
1/4 C. packed brown sugar

3 tbsp red wine vinegar
1 tbsp ketchup
2 C. vegetable oil
3/4 lb medium shrimp - peeled and deveined

Directions

1. Get a small bowl: Mix in it the vanilla wafers, egg, and water. Place the mix in the fridge for 1 h 30 min.
2. Get a small saucepan: Mix in it the nectar with cornstarch. Add the brown sugar, vinegar and ketchup.
3. Place the mix over medium heat and cook them while stirring all the time until it becomes thick to make the sauce. Place it aside.
4. Heat the oil in a large pot or deep fryer until it reaches 375 F. Coat the shrimp with the egg mix then cook it in the hot oil until it becomes golden brown.
5. Drain the shrimp and serve it with the ketchup sauce.
6. Enjoy.

Nori
Noodles Soup

Prep Time: 10 mins
Total Time: 50 mins

Servings per Recipe: 4

Calories	257 kcal
Fat	3.1 g
Carbohydrates	48.2g
Protein	11.6 g
Cholesterol	1 mg
Sodium	1445 mg

Ingredients

1 (8 oz) package dried soba noodles
1 C. prepared dashi stock
1/4 C. soy sauce
2 tbsp mirin
1/4 tsp white sugar

2 tbsp sesame seeds
1/2 C. chopped green onions
1 sheet nori (dried seaweed), cut into thin strips (optional)

Directions

1. Cook the noodles according to the directions on the package. Drain it and cool it down with some water.

2. Place a small saucepan over medium heat. Stir in it the dashi, soy sauce, mirin, and white sugar. Cook it until it starts boiling.

3. Turn off the heat and allow the mix to lose heat for 27 min. Divide the sesame seeds with noodles on serving bowls and pour the stock soup over it.

4. Garnish your soup bowls with the nori and green onions.

5. Enjoy.

HONEY CHILI
and Peanut
Noodles

Prep Time: 15 mins
Total Time: 25 mins

Servings per Recipe: 4
Calories	330 kcal
Fat	12 g
Carbohydrates	46.8g
Protein	10.7 g
Cholesterol	0 mg
Sodium	1188 mg

Ingredients

1/2 C. chicken broth
1 1/2 tbsps minced fresh ginger root
3 tbsps soy sauce
3 tbsps peanut butter
1 1/2 tbsps honey
2 tsps hot chili paste (optional)
3 cloves garlic, minced

8 oz. Udon noodles
1/4 C. chopped green onions
1/4 C. chopped peanuts

Directions

1. Boil your noodles in water for 9 mins then remove all the liquids.
2. At the same time begin to stir and heat the following in a pan: garlic, broth, chili paste, ginger, honey, soy sauce, and peanut butter.
3. Once the mix is hot and smooth add in your noodles when they are finished. Then stir everything to evenly distribute the sauce.
4. Now top the noodles with some peanuts and onions.
5. Enjoy.

Maggie's Easy Coconut Soup

🍲 Prep Time: 35 mins
🕐 Total Time: 1 hr 5 mins

Servings per Recipe: 8
Calories	375 kcal
Fat	33.2 g
Carbohydrates	9.4g
Protein	13.7 g
Cholesterol	89 mg
Sodium	1059 mg

Ingredients

1 tbsp vegetable oil
2 tbsps grated fresh ginger
1 stalk lemon grass, minced
2 tsps red curry paste
4 C. chicken broth
3 tbsps fish sauce
1 tbsp light brown sugar
3 (13.5 oz.) cans coconut milk
1/2 lb fresh shiitake mushrooms, sliced

1 lb medium shrimp - peeled and deveined
2 tbsps fresh lime juice
salt to taste
1/4 C. chopped fresh cilantro

Directions

1. Stir fry your curry paste, lemongrass, and ginger in oil for 2 mins then add in the broth while continuing to stir everything.
2. Add in the brown sugar and fish sauce and let the contents gently boil for 17 mins.
3. Now add the mushrooms and the coconut milk.
4. Continue cooking everything for 7 more min.
5. Then combine in the shrimp and let the fish cook for 7 mins until it is fully done.
6. Now add some cilantro, salt, and lime juice.
7. Enjoy.

PEANUT, Jalapeno, and Cucumber Salad

Prep Time: 15 mins
Total Time: 45 mins

Servings per Recipe: 4
Calories	238 kcal
Fat	9.4 g
Carbohydrates	37.1g
Protein	5.8 g
Cholesterol	O mg
Sodium	1751 mg

Ingredients

3 large cucumbers, peeled, halved lengthwise, seeded, and cut into 1/4-inch slices
1 tbsp salt
1/2 C. white sugar
1/2 C. rice wine vinegar
2 jalapeno peppers, seeded and chopped

1/4 C. chopped cilantro
1/2 C. chopped peanuts

Directions

1. Get a perforated bowl and in the sink combine your salt and cucumbers.
2. Let the mix sit for 40 mins then run the veggies under some fresh water.
3. Now dry everything with some paper towels.
4. Get a bowl, combine: vinegar and sugar.
5. Continue mixing everything until the sugar is fully incorporated with the vinegar then combine in: cilantro, jalapenos, and cucumbers.
6. Top everything with some peanuts.
7. Enjoy.

Catalina's
Spicy Wontons

🥣 Prep Time: 20 mins

🕐 Total Time: 20 mins

Servings per Recipe: 15

Calories	685.4
Fat	66.0g
Cholesterol	26.0mg
Sodium	263.0mg
Carbohydrates	18.9g
Protein	5.8g

Ingredients

1 (8 oz.) packages cream cheese, softened
1 C. Monterey Jack cheese, shredded
1 (4 oz.) cans jalapeño peppers, diced
1 tsp minced garlic
3 green onions, diced

black pepper
1 (16 oz.) packages wonton wrappers
1 quart vegetable oil

Directions

1. In a bowl, add the Monterey Jack cheese, cream cheese, green onions, garlic, jalapeño peppers and black pepper and mix until well combined.
2. Place 1 tsp of the jalapeño mixture in the center of each wonton wrapper.
3. With wet fingers, moisten the edges of each wrapper and then, fold over the filling in a triangle shape.
4. Now, with your fingers, press the edges to seal completely.
5. In a skillet, add the oil over medium-high heat and cook until heated through.
6. Add the wontons in batches and cook until golden brown completely, flipping occasionally.
7. With a slotted spoon, transfer the wrappers onto a paper towel-lined plate to drain.
8. Enjoy.

MANITOBA
Maple Wontons

Prep Time: 15 mins
Total Time: 33 mins

Servings per Recipe: 1
Calories	45.1
Fat	0.1g
Cholesterol	0.7mg
Sodium	83.7mg
Carbohydrates	10.1g
Protein	0.9g

Ingredients

1 C. canned pumpkin
2 tbsp maple syrup
3 tbsp brown sugar
1 tsp pumpkin pie spice
16 packaged wonton wrappers

granulated sugar
ground cinnamon
cooking spray

Directions

1. Set your oven to 400 degrees F before doing anything else.
2. In a bowl, add the pumpkin, pumpkin pie spice, brown sugar and maple syrup and mix until well combined.
3. Place about 1 tbsp of the pumpkin mixture in the center of each wonton wrapper.
4. With wet fingers, moisten the edges of each wrapper and then, fold over the filling in a triangle shape.
5. Now, with your fingers, press the edges to seal completely.
6. In the bottom of an ungreased baking sheet, arrange the wonton wrappers and spray with the cooking spray.
7. Dust the wontons with the cinnamon and granulated sugar and cook in the oven for about 16 minutes.
8. Carefully, flip the side and cook in the oven for about 2 minutes.
9. Remove from the oven and keep aside to cool.
10. Enjoy.

Silver Dragon
Wonton Soup

Prep Time: 20 mins
Total Time: 28 mins

Servings per Recipe: 6
Calories	123.1
Fat	3.5g
Cholesterol	13.7mg
Sodium	973.7mg
Carbohydrates	11.2g
Protein	10.4g

Ingredients

2 green onions
1/4 lb. lean ground beef
1/4 C. chopped celery
1 tbsp chopped parsley
1/4 tsp salt
1 dash pepper

12 - 18 wonton skins
6 C. chicken broth
1/2 C. spinach, shredded
1/4 C. shredded carrot

Directions

1. Remove the top from 1 green onion and cut into thin slices diagonally.
2. Reserve the slices for garnishing.
3. Then, cut the remaining green onions into small pieces.
4. In a bowl, add the ground beef, celery, chopped onion, parsley, salt and pepper and gently, stir to combine.
5. Place about 1 1/2 tbsp of the beef mixture in the center of each wonton square.
6. With wet fingers, moisten the edges of each wrapper and then, fold over the filling in a triangle shape.
7. Now, with your fingers, press the edges to seal completely.
8. In a pan, add the broth and cook until boiling.
9. Now, set the heat to medium.
10. Add the wontons in 2 batches and cook for about 4 minutes.
11. With a slotted spoon, transfer the wontons onto a plate and with a piece of foil, cover them to keep warm.
12. In hot broth, add the spinach, carrot and reserved green onion slices and stir to combine.
13. Divide the wontons into serving bowls and top with the hot broth mixture.
14. Enjoy hot.

ARTISANAL
Wonton Tins

Prep Time: 30 mins
Total Time: 1 hr

Servings per Recipe: 48
Calories   67.3
Fat   3.4g
Cholesterol   7.4mg
Sodium   141.5mg
Carbohydrates   6.5g
Protein   2.8g

Ingredients

1 C. freshly grated Parmesan cheese
1 C. mayonnaise
1/2 tsp onion powder
1/2 tsp garlic powder
2 C. shredded mozzarella cheese

1 (14 oz.) cans water-packed artichoke hearts, drained and chopped
1 (12 oz.) packages wonton wrappers

Directions

1. Set your oven to 350 degrees F before doing anything else.
2. In a bowl, add the mayonnaise, Parmesan cheese, garlic powder and onion powder and mix until blended nicely.
3. Add the artichoke pieces and mozzarella cheese and mix well.
4. With the cooking spray, spray one side of all wonton wrappers.
5. Place 1 wrapper into 1 of each mini muffin C. and press to fit in a C. shape.
6. Cook in the oven for about 5 minutes.
7. Remove from the oven and place 1 tbsp of the artichoke mixture in each C..
8. Cook in the oven for about 5-6 minutes.
9. Enjoy warm.

How to Make
Wonton Wraps

🥣 Prep Time: 1 hr 30 mins
🕐 Total Time: 1 hr 30 mins

Servings per Recipe: 1
Calories	981.5
Fat	7.2g
Cholesterol	186.0mg
Sodium	1242.3mg
Carbohydrates	191.1g
Protein	32.1g

Ingredients

2 C. all-purpose flour
1/2 tsp salt
1 egg
1/4 C. water

1/4 C. water
extra flour

Directions

1. In a bowl, add the flour and salt and mix well.
2. In another bowl, add the egg and 1/4 C. of water and gently, beat until well combined.
3. With your hands, create a well in the center of the flour mixture.
4. Add the egg mixture in the well and mix alongside the remaining water.
5. With your hands, knead the dough until a smooth dough forms.
6. Transfer the dough into a bowl.
7. With a damp cloth, cover the bowl and aside for about 1 hour.
8. Divide the dough into 4 equal sized portions.
9. Place one dough portion onto a generously floured surface and with a rolling pin, roll into a very thin circle.
10. Now, cut the dough into equal sized circles.
11. Repeat with the remaining dough portions.

Printed in Great Britain
by Amazon